The Brothers Grimm

The Town Musicians of Bremen

The Brothers Grimm

The Town Musicians of Bremen

Illustrated
by Volker Ernsting

Lappan

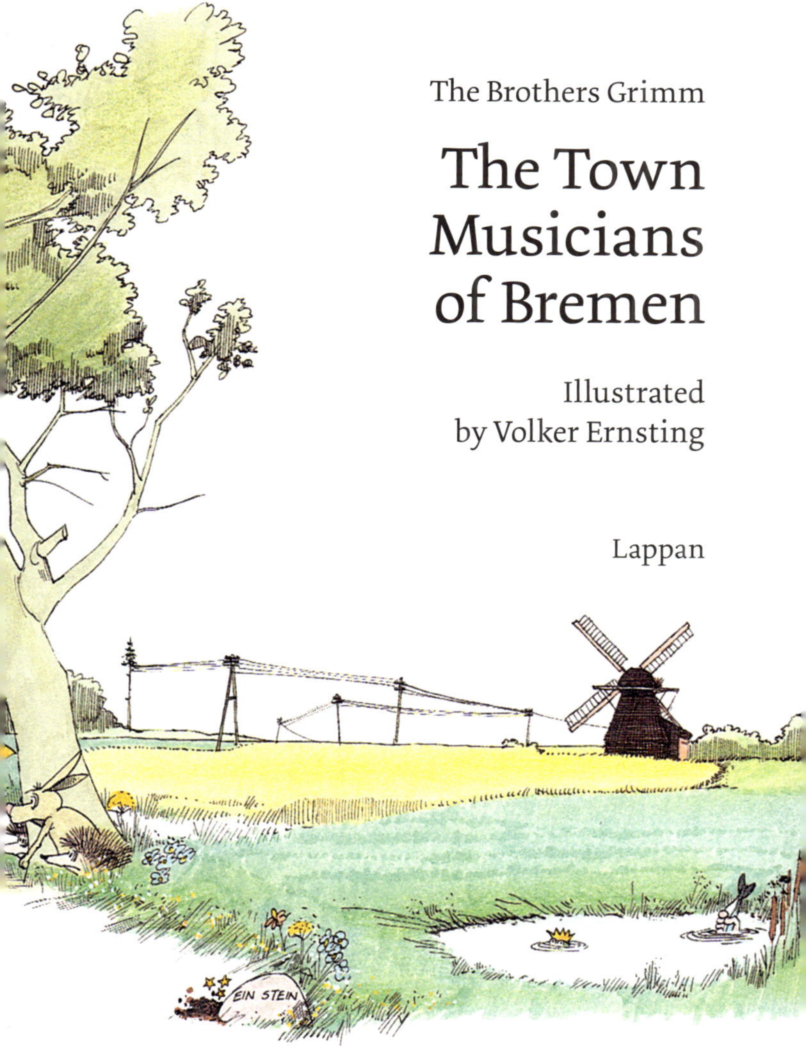

There was once a man who kept a donkey. Year after year the poor beast carried heavy sacks to the mill, never flagging or complaining. But then his strength began to run out and slowly

but surely the work became too much for him. So it was that his master started to wonder why he should go on feeding him. But the donkey knew that the future looked bleak ...

So he ran away and set off towards Bremen thinking
that he could perhaps become a town musician.

Bremen 2 Tage

He had not gone far before he came across a hunting dog lying at the side of the road yapping away as if he had just run so far that he was too tired to take another step.

"Now then, old dog, why are you barking so sadly?" asked the donkey. "Oh dear", said the dog, "you see, because I'm old and getting weaker every day, I can't go hunting any more. My master was going to kill me, so I took to my heels; but how can I earn my living now?"

"Do you know what?" said the donkey, "I'm on my way to Bremen and I'm going to become a town musician there. Why don't you come with me and take up music as well. I'll play the lute, and you can play the drums."

The dog agreed and they set off together.

They had not gone much further when they saw a cat sitting by the wayside with a face as long as three rainy days.

"Well now, what's getting you down, old furry friend?" asked the donkey.

"It's difficult to be cheerful when your life is at stake", answered the cat. "You see, I'm not so young as I used to be and my teeth are getting blunt, so I prefer to sit and purr in front of the fire rather than go chasing after mice. That's why my mistress made up her mind to drown me; so of course I ran away, but who can tell me where I should go now?"

"Why not come with us to Bremen? You know all about night music, so you can become a town musician."

The cat thought this sounded a good idea and tagged along.

Tietjen

A while later, as the three refugees were going past a farmyard, they saw a cock sitting on the gate crowing for all he was worth.
"What's all this?" said the donkey. "Your crowing is enough to give anyone a headache."
"I was announcing that the weather is going to be fine", the cock replied, "because today is the day of Our Blessed Lady, when she washed the baby Jesus's little shirt and wanted to dry it.
But tomorrow we are having guests for

Sunday dinner and the farmer's wife has no pity: she's told the cook to put me in the soup. My head is going to be chopped off this evening, so now I'm crowing at the top of my voice while I still can."
"Where's the sense in that, old feathered friend?" said the donkey. "Why not come with us instead, we're on our way to Bremen. You can always find something better than dying wherever you go; you've got a good voice and if we all play together it's bound to be a success."

The cock agreed to join them and all four continued on their way together.

But the town of Bremen was too far to reach in a single day so, when evening fell, they decided to spend the night in a forest.

The donkey and the dog laid down under a big tree while the cat and the cock made themselves at home in the branches. The cock flew to the very top of the tree, where he felt safest and before settling down to sleep he took a last look around him in every direction. Suddenly he thought he could see a glimmer of light in the distance and so he called down to his friends saying: "I can see a light shining, there must be a house not too far away." The donkey answered: "Then let's see if we can find it, after all it's not very comfortable here", and the dog added that he could

also do with a couple of bones with a bit of meat on them. So together they set off in the direction of the light and soon it became brighter and grew even larger until they found themselves standing in front of a robbers' house with the lights burning brightly.

Priesporter
Schwalmen-
geist
KÖHNE
KETCHUP

The donkey, being the tallest of the four, crept up to the window and peered inside.
"What can you see, old grey ears?" asked the cock.
"I'll tell you what I can see", answered the donkey, "there's a table full of good things to eat and drink and some robbers sitting round it enjoying themselves."
"That's just what we need", said the cock.
"Yes indeed, if only there was some way to get at all that food!" agreed the donkey.

So the animals all put their heads together and at last they came up with a way of frightening the robbers out of the house. This is what they did:

The donkey put his front hooves up on the window-sill,

then the dog jumped up on the donkey's back,

the cat climbed onto the dog,

and last of all the cock flew up
and sat on the cat's head.

Once that was done, the donkey
gave a signal and together they
set up a deafening chorus: the
donkey brayed, the dog barked, the
cat miaowed and the cock crowed.

Then they burst through the window into the room sending a shower of glass clattering to the floor. Hearing the awful din, the robbers lept out of their chairs thinking that a ghost had come to them, and they fled in terror out into the forest.

Now the four friends sat down at the table and started to devour what was left on the tables as if they might not eat again for a month.

When they had eaten their fill, the four musicians put out the light and each one found himself a corner to sleep in which suited him best. The donkey laid down on some old straw, the dog behind the door, the cat on the hearth near the warm ashes and the cock perched on a beam under the roof; and tired as they were after their long journey, it did not take long before they were all fast asleep.

When it was past midnight the robbers could see from the distance that there was no light burning in the house and everything seemed quiet. The leader of the gang said: "We should never have let ourselves be frightened away like that", and he ordered one of the robbers to go and take a look in the house.

The robber found everything perfectly still and went into the kitchen to light a candle. Seeing the cat's fiery eyes shining in the dark, he took them for glowing coals and pushed a sulphur match towards them to light it. But the cat was not at all amused and jumped into his face scratching and spitting.

The robber got the shock of his life, and when he tried to escape out of the back door, the dog, who was lying there, jumped up and bit him in the leg. Then, as he ran across the yard past the pile of old straw, the donkey gave him a hearty kick with his rear hoof.

By this time the cock had been woken up by all the goings-on and crowed cheerfully from his beam: "Cock-a-doodle-do!"

The robber ran for all he was worth back to his leader and said: "It's terrible, there's a gruesome old witch in the house – she spat at me and scratched my face with her long fingernails; and there's a man standing behind the door with a knife who stabbed me in the leg; then outside in the yard there's a black monster which set about me

with a wooden club; and the judge was sitting up on the roof and shouted: 'Bring the scoundrel here!' So I didn't wait to see any more."

From that moment onwards the robbers did not dare to set foot in the house ever again – but the four Town Musicians of Bremen felt so at home that they never wanted to leave.

FCK

verden
Bremen
Oldenburg
HB-1985

ISBN 978-3-8303-1169-0

13. Auflage 2013

Originaltitel: Die Bremer Stadtmusikanten

www.lappan.de

Der Lappan Verlag ist ein Unternehmen
der Verlagsgruppe Ueberreuter.